MW00910703

2013

Personal Data **Persönliche Daten** **Información Personal**
Dati Personali **Informations Personnelles** **Persoonlijke Gegevens**

Name Name Nom Nome Nombre Naam

Address Adresse Adresse Indirizzo Dirección Adres

Tel / Mobile

Fax

E-mail

www

Company Firma Société Ditta Compañía Bedrijf

Address Adresse Adresse Indirizzo Dirección Adres

Tel / Mobile

Fax

E-mail

www

Notes Notizen Notes Note Apuntes Notities

World Time Differences Internationale Zeitunterschiede Fuseaux horaires
Fusi Orari Diferencias De Horas Internacionales International Tijdsverschiller

Abu Dhabi	+4	Freetown	0	Port-au-Prince	-5
Accra	0	Geneva	+1	Prague	+1
Addis Ababa	+3	Glasgow	0	Pyongyang	+9
Alexandria	+2	Halifax	-4	Rangoon	+6$\frac{1}{2}$
Algiers	+1	Harare	+2	Reykjavik	0
Amman	+2	Havana	-5	Rio de Janeiro	-3
Amsterdam	+1	Helsinki	+2	Riyadh	+3
Anchorage	-9	Ho Chi Minh	+7	Rome	+1
Antigua (St. John's)	-4	Hong Kong	+8	San Juan	-4
Athens	+2	Honolulu	-10	Santiago	-4
Atlanta	-5	Houston	-6	Sao Paulo	-3
Auckland	+12	Istanbul	+2	Sarajevo	+1
Azores	-1	Jakarta	+7	Saskatchewan (Regina)	-6
Baghdad	+3	Jerusalem	+2	Seoul	+9
Baku	+4	Johannesburg	+2	Shanghai	+8
Bangkok	+7	Kabul	+4$\frac{1}{2}$	Singapore	+8
Barcelona	+1	Karachi	+5	Sofia	+2
Basra	+3	Kathmandu	+5$\frac{3}{4}$	St. Louis	-6
Beijing	+8	Khartoum	+3	St. Petersburg	+3
Beirut	+2	Kuala Lumpur	+8	Stockholm	+1
Belfast	0	Kuwait City	+3	Sydney	+10
Belize City	-6	Lagos	+1	Taipei	+8
Berlin	+1	La Paz	-4	Tehran	+3$\frac{1}{2}$
Bern	+1	Lima	-5	Timbuktu	0
Bogota	-5	Lisbon	0	Tokyo	+9
Bombay	+5$\frac{1}{2}$	Ljubljana	+1	Toronto	-5
Brussels	+1	London	0	Tunis	+1
Budapest	+1	Los Angeles	-8	Ulaan Baator	+8
Buenos Aires	-3	Madrid	+1	Vancouver	-8
Cairo	+2	Managua	-6	Vienna	+1
Calcutta	+5$\frac{1}{2}$	Manila	+8	Vladivostok	+10
Calgary	-7	Martinique		Volgograd	+3
Caracas	-4	(Fort-de-France)	-4	Warsaw	+1
Casablanca	0	Melbourne	+10	Winnipeg	-6
Chicago	-6	Mexico City	-6	Yokohama	+9
Copenhagen	+1	Mogadishu	+3	Zurich	+1
Curaçao	-4	Montevideo	-3		
Dakar	0	Montreal	-5		
Damascus	+2	Moscow	+3		
Dar-es-Salaam	+3	Nairobi	+3		
Denver	-7	New Delhi	+5$\frac{1}{2}$		
Dublin	0	New York	-5		
Edinburgh	0	Oslo	+1		
Edmonton	-7	Ottawa	-5		
Frankfurt	+1	Paris	+1		

* Please note that the above numbers are according to Winter Standard Time. For those countries which participate in Daylight Saving Time, please add one hour during the summer months. Time differences added/subtracted from GMT (Greenwich Mean Time).

International Dialing Codes Internationale Vorwahlnummern Codes Internationaux

from \ to	(A)	(B)	(DK)	(F)	(D)	(GB)	(GR)	(I)	(L)	(NL)	(N)	(P)	(E)	(CH)	(USA)
(A)	·	00-32	00-45	00-33	00-49	00-44	00-30	00-39	00-352	00-31	00-47	00-351	00-34	00-41	00-1
(B)	00-43	·	00-45	00-33	00-49	00-44	00-30	00-39	00-352	00-31	00-47	00-351	00-34	00-41	00-1
(DK)	00-43	00-32	·	00-33	00-49	00-44	00-30	00-39	00-352	00-31	00-47	00-351	00-34	00-41	00-1
(F)	00-43	00-32	00-45	·	00-49	00-44	00-30	00-39	00-352	00-31	00-47	00-351	00-34	00-41	00-1
(D)	00-43	00-32	00-45	00-33	·	00-44	00-30	00-39	00-352	00-31	00-47	00-351	00-34	00-41	00-1
(GB)	00-43	00-32	00-45	00-33	00-49	·	00-30	00-39	00-352	00-31	00-47	00-351	00-34	00-41	00-1
(GR)	00-43	00-32	00-45	00-33	00-49	00-44	·	00-39	00-352	00-31	00-47	00-351	00-34	00-41	00-1
(I)	00-43	00-32	00-45	00-33	00-49	00-44	00-30	·	00-352	00-31	00-47	00-351	00-34	00-41	00-1
(L)	00-43	00-32	00-45	00-33	00-49	00-44	00-30	00-39	·	00-31	00-47	00-351	00-34	00-41	00-1
(NL)	00-43	00-32	00-45	00-33	00-49	00-44	00-30	00-39	00-352	·	00-47	00-351	00-34	00-41	00-1
(N)	00-43	00-32	00-45	00-33	00-49	00-44	00-30	00-39	00-352	00-31	·	00-351	00-34	00-41	00-1
(P)	00-43	00-32	00-45	00-33	00-49	00-44	00-30	00-39	00-352	00-31	00-47	·	00-34	00-41	00-1
(E)	00-43	00-32	00-45	00-33	00-49	00-44	00-30	00-39	00-352	00-31	00-47	00-351	·	00-41	00-1
(CH)	00-43	00-32	00-45	00-33	00-49	00-44	00-30	00-39	00-352	00-31	00-47	00-351	00-34	·	00-1
(USA)	011-43	011-32	011-45	011-33	011-49	011-44	011-30	011-39	011-352	011-31	011-47	011-351	011-34	011-41	·

"To place an international telephone call, dial the international access code (e.g. 011 in U.S.), the country code number, and then the local number." "without guarantee"

1	Thu	
2	Fri	
3	Sat	
4	Sun	
5	Mon	Week 45
6	Tue	
7	Wed	
8	Thu	
9	Fri	
10	Sat	
11	Sun	
12	Mon	Week 46
13	Tue	
14	Wed	
15	Thu	
16	Fri	
17	Sat	
18	Sun	
19	Mon	Week 47
20	Tue	
21	Wed	
22	Thu	
23	Fri	
24	Sat	
25	Sun	
26	Mon	Week 48
27	Tue	
28	Wed	
29	Thu	
30	Fri	

1	Sat	
2	Sun	
3	Mon	Week 49
4	Tue	
5	Wed	
6	Thu	☾
7	Fri	
8	Sat	
9	Sun	
10	Mon	Week 50
11	Tue	
12	Wed	
13	Thu	●
14	Fri	
15	Sat	
16	Sun	
17	Mon	Week 51
18	Tue	
19	Wed	
20	Thu	☽
21	Fri	
22	Sat	
23	Sun	
24	Mon	Week 52
25	Tue	
26	Wed	
27	Thu	
28	Fri	○
29	Sat	
30	Sun	
31	Mon	Week 1

1	Tue	Week 1	
2	Wed		
3	Thu		
4	Fri		
5	Sat		☾
6	Sun		
7	Mon	Week 2	
8	Tue		
9	Wed		
10	Thu		
11	Fri		●
12	Sat		
13	Sun		
14	Mon	Week 3	
15	Tue		
16	Wed		
17	Thu		
18	Fri		☽
19	Sat		
20	Sun		
21	Mon	Week 4	
22	Tue		
23	Wed		
24	Thu		
25	Fri		
26	Sat		
27	Sun		○
28	Mon	Week 5	
29	Tue		
30	Wed		
31	Thu		

1	Fri	
2	Sat	
3	Sun	☾
4	Mon	Week 6
5	Tue	
6	Wed	
7	Thu	
8	Fri	
9	Sat	
10	Sun	●
11	Mon	Week 7
12	Tue	
13	Wed	
14	Thu	
15	Fri	
16	Sat	
17	Sun	☽
18	Mon	Week 8
19	Tue	
20	Wed	
21	Thu	
22	Fri	
23	Sat	
24	Sun	
25	Mon	Week 9 ○
26	Tue	
27	Wed	
28	Thu	

1	Fri	
2	Sat	
3	Sun	
4	Mon	Week 10	☾
5	Tue	
6	Wed	
7	Thu	
8	Fri	
9	Sat	
10	Sun	
11	Mon	Week 11	●
12	Tue	
13	Wed	
14	Thu	
15	Fri	
16	Sat	
17	Sun	
18	Mon	Week 12	
19	Tue	☽
20	Wed	
21	Thu	
22	Fri	
23	Sat	
24	Sun	
25	Mon	Week 13	
26	Tue	
27	Wed	○
28	Thu	
29	Fri	
30	Sat	
31	Sun	

1	Mon	Week 14	
2	Tue		
3	Wed		☾
4	Thu		
5	Fri		
6	Sat		
7	Sun		
8	Mon	Week 15	
9	Tue		
10	Wed		●
11	Thu		
12	Fri		
13	Sat		
14	Sun		
15	Mon	Week 16	
16	Tue		
17	Wed		
18	Thu		☽
19	Fri		
20	Sat		
21	Sun		
22	Mon	Week 17	
23	Tue		
24	Wed		
25	Thu		○
26	Fri		
27	Sat		
28	Sun		
29	Mon	Week 18	
30	Tue		

1	Wed	
2	Thu	
3	Fri	
4	Sat	
5	Sun	
6	Mon	Week 19
7	Tue	
8	Wed	
9	Thu	
10	Fri	
11	Sat	
12	Sun	
13	Mon	Week 20
14	Tue	
15	Wed	
16	Thu	
17	Fri	
18	Sat	
19	Sun	
20	Mon	Week 21
21	Tue	
22	Wed	
23	Thu	
24	Fri	
25	Sat	
26	Sun	
27	Mon	Week 22
28	Tue	
29	Wed	
30	Thu	
31	Fri	

1	Sat	
2	Sun	
3	Mon	Week 23
4	Tue	
5	Wed	
6	Thu	
7	Fri	
8	Sat	●
9	Sun	
10	Mon	Week 24
11	Tue	
12	Wed	
13	Thu	
14	Fri	
15	Sat	
16	Sun	☽
17	Mon	Week 25
18	Tue	
19	Wed	
20	Thu	
21	Fri	
22	Sat	
23	Sun	○
24	Mon	Week 26
25	Tue	
26	Wed	
27	Thu	
28	Fri	
29	Sat	
30	Sun	☾

1	Mon	Week 27
2	Tue	
3	Wed	
4	Thu	
5	Fri	
6	Sat	
7	Sun	
8	Mon	Week 28
9	Tue	
10	Wed	
11	Thu	
12	Fri	
13	Sat	
14	Sun	
15	Mon	Week 29
16	Tue	
17	Wed	
18	Thu	
19	Fri	
20	Sat	
21	Sun	
22	Mon	Week 30
23	Tue	
24	Wed	
25	Thu	
26	Fri	
27	Sat	
28	Sun	
29	Mon	Week 31
30	Tue	
31	Wed	

1	Thu	
2	Fri	
3	Sat	
4	Sun	
5	Mon	Week 32
6	Tue	●
7	Wed	
8	Thu	
9	Fri	
10	Sat	
11	Sun	
12	Mon	Week 33
13	Tue	
14	Wed	
15	Thu	
16	Fri	
17	Sat	
18	Sun	
19	Mon	Week 34
20	Tue	
21	Wed	○
22	Thu	
23	Fri	
24	Sat	
25	Sun	
26	Mon	Week 35
27	Tue	
28	Wed	☾
29	Thu	
30	Fri	
31	Sat	

1	Sun	
2	Mon	Week 36
3	Tue	
4	Wed	
5	Thu	●
6	Fri	
7	Sat	
8	Sun	
9	Mon	Week 37
10	Tue	
11	Wed	
12	Thu	☽
13	Fri	
14	Sat	
15	Sun	
16	Mon	Week 38
17	Tue	
18	Wed	
19	Thu	○
20	Fri	
21	Sat	
22	Sun	
23	Mon	Week 39
24	Tue	
25	Wed	
26	Thu	
27	Fri	☾
28	Sat	
29	Sun	
30	Mon	Week 40

1	Tue	
2	Wed	
3	Thu	
4	Fri	
5	Sat	●
6	Sun	
7	Mon	Week 41
8	Tue	
9	Wed	
10	Thu	
11	Fri	☽
12	Sat	
13	Sun	
14	Mon	Week 42
15	Tue	
16	Wed	
17	Thu	
18	Fri	○
19	Sat	
20	Sun	
21	Mon	Week 43
22	Tue	
23	Wed	
24	Thu	
25	Fri	
26	Sat	☾
27	Sun	
28	Mon	Week 44
29	Tue	
30	Wed	
31	Thu	

1	Fri	
2	Sat	
3	Sun	●
4	Mon	Week 45
5	Tue	
6	Wed	
7	Thu	
8	Fri	
9	Sat	
10	Sun	☽
11	Mon	Week 46
12	Tue	
13	Wed	
14	Thu	
15	Fri	
16	Sat	
17	Sun	○
18	Mon	Week 47
19	Tue	
20	Wed	
21	Thu	
22	Fri	
23	Sat	
24	Sun	
25	Mon	Week 48 ☾
26	Tue	
27	Wed	
28	Thu	
29	Fri	
30	Sat	

2013 DECEMBER DICIEMBRE DICEMBRE DÉCEMBRE DEZEMBER **DECEMBER**

1	Sun	
2	Mon	Week 49
3	Tue	●
4	Wed	
5	Thu	
6	Fri	
7	Sat	
8	Sun	
9	Mon	Week 50
10	Tue	
11	Wed	
12	Thu	
13	Fri	
14	Sat	
15	Sun	
16	Mon	Week 51
17	Tue	○
18	Wed	
19	Thu	
20	Fri	
21	Sat	
22	Sun	
23	Mon	Week 52
24	Tue	
25	Wed	☾
26	Thu	
27	Fri	
28	Sat	
29	Sun	
30	Mon	Week 1
31	Tue	

Holiday List Feiertage Jours Fériés Giorni Festivi Dias Festivos Feestdagen 2013

December 2012
December 26, 2012, Wednesday
Boxing Day, *Australia, Canada, New Zealand, UK*
Kwanzaa begins, *USA*
St. Stephen's Day • Stephanitag •
Stephanstag • 2. Weihnachtstag •
Tweede kerstdag
Bank Holiday, *UK*

December 31, 2012, Monday
New Year's Eve • Silvester •
Saint-Sylvestre • Oudejaarsavond

January 2013
January 1, 2013, Tuesday
Kwanzaa ends, *USA*
New Year's Day • Neujahr •
Nouvel An • Nieuwjaar

January 2, 2013, Wednesday
Berchtoldstag, *Switzerland*
Bank Holiday, *Scotland*

January 6, 2013, Sunday
Epiphany • Heilige Drei Könige •
Epiphanie • Driekoningen

January 21, 2013, Monday
Martin Luther King, Jr.'s Birthday,
USA

January 25, 2013, Friday
Robert Burns Day, *Scotland*
Tou Bichvat • Tu Bishvat
(begins at sundown)

January 26, 2013, Saturday
Australia Day, *Australia*

January 31, 2013, Thursday
Koningin Beatrix (1938), *Netherlands*

February 2013
February 6, 2013, Wednesday
Waitangi Day, *New Zealand*

February 10, 2013, Sunday
Chinese (Lunar) New Year

February 11, 2013, Monday
Rosenmontag, *Germany*

February 12, 2013, Tuesday
Fastnacht, *Germany*
Shrove Tuesday • Mardi Gras,
Canada, France, USA

February 13, 2013, Wednesday
Ash Wednesday • Aschermittwoch •
Cendres • Aswoensdag

February 14, 2013, Thursday
St. Valentine's Day • Valentinstag •
Saint-Valentin • Valentijnsdag

February 18, 2013, Monday
Washington's Birthday
(President's Day), *USA*

February 23, 2013, Saturday
Pourim • Purim (begins at sundown)

March 2013
March 1, 2013, Friday
St. David's Day, *Wales*

March 10, 2013, Sunday
Daylight Saving Time begins,
Canada, USA
Mothering Sunday
(Mother's Day), *UK*

March 17, 2013, Sunday
St. Patrick's Day, *N. Ireland,
Rep. of Ireland, USA*

March 19, 2013, Tuesday
Josephstag, *Switzerland*

March 20, 2013, Wednesday
Vernal Equinox • Frühlings-
Tagundnachtgleiche • Printemps
(11:02 Universal Time)

March 24, 2013, Sunday
Palm Sunday • Palmsonntag •
Dimanche des Rameaux •
Palmzondag

March 25, 2013, Monday
Pessa'h • Pesach
(begins at sundown)

March 28, 2013, Thursday
Gründonnerstag, *Germany*
Witte Donderdag, *Belgium,
Netherlands*

March 29, 2013, Friday
Good Friday • Karfreitag •
Vendredi Saint • Goede Vrijdag
Bank Holiday, *UK*

March 31, 2013, Sunday
Easter Sunday • Ostersonntag •
Pâques • Pasen
Clocks forward one hour, *UK*
Begin zomertijd, *Belgium,
Netherlands*
Beginn der Sommerzeit, *Austria,
Germany, Switzerland*

April 2013
April 1, 2013, Monday
Easter Monday • Ostermontag •
Lundi de Pâques • Tweede paasdag
Bank Holiday, *UK*

April 6, 2013, Saturday
Yom HaShoah (Holocaust Remembrance Day – begins at sundown)

April 15, 2013, Monday
Yom Ha'atzmaout • Yom HaAtzmaut
(begins at sundown)

April 23, 2013, Tuesday
St. George's Day, *England*

April 25, 2013, Thursday
Anzac Day, *Australia, New Zealand*

April 27, 2013, Saturday
Prins Willem Alexander (1967),
Netherlands
Lag BaOmer (begins at sundown)

April 30, 2013, Tuesday
Koninginnedag, *Netherlands*

May 2013
May 1, 2013, Wednesday
Dag van de Arbeid, *Netherlands*
Feest van de Arbeid, *Belgium*
Fête du travail, *France*
Maifeiertag, *Germany*
Staatsfeiertag, *Austria*
Tag der Arbeit, *Switzerland*

May 4, 2013, Saturday
Herdenking der gevallenen,
Netherlands

May 5, 2013, Sunday
Bevrijdingsdag, *Netherlands*

May 6, 2013, Monday
May Day Bank Holiday, *UK,
Rep. of Ireland, Australia*

May 8, 2013, Wednesday
Fête de la Victoire 1945, *France*

May 9, 2013, Thursday
Ascension Day • Christi Himmel-
fahrt • Ascension •
Hemelvaartsdag • Auffahrt

May 12, 2013, Sunday
Mother's Day • Muttertag •
Moederdag

May 14, 2013, Tuesday
Chavouoth • Shavuot
(begins at sundown)

May 19, 2013, Sunday
Pentecost Sunday • Pfingstsonntag • Pentecôte • Pinksteren

May 20, 2013, Monday
Pentecost Monday • Pfingst-
montag • Lundi de Pentecôte •
Tweede pinksterdag
Victoria Day, *Canada*

May 26, 2013, Sunday
Fête des Mères, *France*

May 27, 2013, Monday
Memorial Day, *USA*
Spring Bank Holiday, *UK*

May 30, 2013, Thursday
Fronleichnam, *Austria,
Germany, Switzerland*

June 2013
June 3, 2013, Monday
Queen's Birthday, *New Zealand*
Bank Holiday, *Rep. of Ireland*

June 16, 2013, Sunday
Father's Day • Fête des Pères •
Vaderdag

June 21, 2013, Friday
Summer Solstice • Sommer-
sonnenwende • Solstice d'été
(05:04 Universal Time)

2013 Feestdagen Dias Festivos Giorni Festivi Jours Fériés Feiertage Holiday List

June 24, 2013, Monday
St. Jean Baptiste Day, Canada
(Quebec)

July 2013
July 1, 2013, Monday
Canada Day, Canada

July 4, 2013, Thursday
Independence Day, USA

July 12, 2013, Friday
Battle of the Boyne
(Orangemen's Day), N. Ireland

July 14, 2013, Sunday
Fête Nationale, France

July 15, 2013, Monday
Tisha Beav · Tisha B'Av
(begins at sundown)

July 21, 2013, Sunday
Nationale Feestdag /
Fête Nationale, Belgium

August 2013
August 1, 2013, Thursday
Nationalfeiertag, Switzerland

August 5, 2013, Monday
Summer Bank Holiday,
Rep. of Ireland, Scotland

August 15, 2013, Thursday
Feast of the Assumption ·
Mariä Himmelfahrt · Assomption ·
Maria-Tenhemelopneming

August 26, 2013, Monday
Summer Bank Holiday, UK
(except Scotland)

September 2013
September 2, 2013, Monday
Labor Day, USA
Labour Day, Canada

September 4, 2013, Wednesday
Roch Hachana · Rosh HaShana
(begins at sundown)

September 13, 2013, Friday
Yom Kippour · Yom Kippur
(begins at sundown)

September 15, 2013, Sunday
Eidgenössische Dank-, Buß- und
Bettag, Switzerland

September 18, 2013, Wednesday
Souccot · Sukkot (begins at sundown)

September 21, 2013, Saturday
U.N. International Day of Peace

September 22, 2013, Sunday
Autumnal Equinox · Herbst-
Tagundnachtgleiche · Automne
(20:44 Universal Time)

September 25, 2013, Wednesday
Chemini Atseret · Shmini Atzeret
(begins at sundown)

September 26, 2013, Thursday
Sim'hat Torah · Simchat Torah
(begins at sundown)

October 2013
October 3, 2013, Thursday
Tag der Deutschen Einheit, Germany

October 6, 2013, Sunday
Erntedankfest, Germany

October 14, 2013, Monday
Columbus Day, USA
Thanksgiving Day, Canada

October 26, 2013, Saturday
Nationalfeiertag, Austria

October 27, 2013, Sunday
Clocks back one hour, UK
Einde zomertijd, Belgium,
Netherlands
Ende der Sommerzeit, Austria,
Germany, Switzerland

October 28, 2013, Monday
Bank Holiday, Rep. of Ireland
Labour Day, New Zealand

October 31, 2013, Thursday
Reformationstag, Germany
Halloween, USA, UK

November 2013
November 1, 2013, Friday
All Saints' Day · Allerheiligen ·
Toussaint

November 2, 2013, Saturday
Allerseelen, Austria
Allerzielen, Belgium, Netherlands

November 3, 2013, Sunday
Daylight Saving Time ends, USA,
Canada

November 5, 2013, Tuesday
Election Day, USA

November 10, 2013, Sunday
Remembrance Sunday, UK

November 11, 2013, Monday
Martinstag, Germany
Armistice of 1918
(Jour du Souvenir), France
Remembrance Day, Canada,
Australia
Veteran's Day, USA
Wapenstilstand 1918, Belgium

November 17, 2013, Sunday
Volkstrauertag, Germany

November 20, 2013, Wednesday
Buß- und Bettag, Germany

November 24, 2013, Sunday
Totensonntag, Germany
Ewigkeitssonntag, Austria

November 27, 2013, Wednesday
Hanoucca · Chanukkah
(begins at sundown)

November 28, 2013, Thursday
Thanksgiving Day, USA

November 30, 2013, Saturday
St. Andrew's Day, Scotland

December 2013
December 2, 2013, Monday
Bank Holiday, Scotland

December 5, 2013, Thursday
Sinterklaasavond, Netherlands

December 6, 2013, Friday
Saint-Nicolas, France
Sinterklaas, Netherlands

December 8, 2013, Sunday
Immaculate Conception · Mariä
Empfängnis · Immaculée Conception
· Maria-Onbevlekte-Ontvangenis

December 21, 2013, Saturday
Winter Solstice · Wintersonnen-
wende · Solstice d'hiver
(17:11 Universal Time)

December 24, 2013, Tuesday
Christmas Eve · Heiligabend ·
Veille de Noël · Kerstavond

December 25, 2013, Wednesday
Christmas Day · 1. Weihnachtstag ·
Noël · Kerstmis
Bank Holiday, UK

December 26, 2013, Thursday
Boxing Day, Australia, Canada,
New Zealand, UK
Kwanzaa begins, USA
St. Stephen's Day · Stephanitag ·
Stephanstag · 2. Weihnachtstag ·
Tweede kerstdag
Bank Holiday, UK

December 31, 2013, Tuesday
New Year's Eve · Silvester ·
Saint-Sylvestre · Oudejaarsavond

January 2014
January 1, 2014, Wednesday
Kwanzaa ends, USA
New Year's Day · Neujahr ·
Nouvel An · Nieuwjaar
Bank Holiday, UK

January 2, 2014, Thursday
Berchtoldstag, Switzerland
Bank Holiday, Scotland

January 6, 2014, Monday
Epiphany · Heilige Drei Könige ·
Epiphanie · Driekoningen

January 2013

M	T	W	T	F	S	S
	1	2	3	4	5	6
7	8	9	10	11	12	13
14	15	16	17	18	19	20
21	22	23	24	25	26	27
28	29	30	31			

February 2013

M	T	W	T	F	S	S
				1	2	3
4	5	6	7	8	9	10
11	12	13	14	15	16	17
18	19	20	21	22	23	24
25	26	27	28			

March 2013

M	T	W	T	F	S	S
				1	2	3
4	5	6	7	8	9	10
11	12	13	14	15	16	17
18	19	20	21	22	23	24
25	26	27	28	29	30	31

April 2013

M	T	W	T	F	S	S
1	2	3	4	5	6	7
8	9	10	11	12	13	14
15	16	17	18	19	20	21
22	23	24	25	26	27	28
29	30					

May 2013

M	T	W	T	F	S	S
	1	2	3	4	5	
6	7	8	9	10	11	12
13	14	15	16	17	18	19
20	21	22	23	24	25	26
27	28	29	30	31		

June 2013

M	T	W	T	F	S	S
					1	2
3	4	5	6	7	8	9
10	11	12	13	14	15	16
17	18	19	20	21	22	23
24	25	26	27	28	29	30

July 2013

M	T	W	T	F	S	S
1	2	3	4	5	6	7
8	9	10	11	12	13	14
15	16	17	18	19	20	21
22	23	24	25	26	27	28
29	30	31				

August 2013

M	T	W	T	F	S	S
			1	2	3	4
5	6	7	8	9	10	11
12	13	14	15	16	17	18
19	20	21	22	23	24	25
26	27	28	29	30	31	

September 2013

M	T	W	T	F	S	S
						1
2	3	4	5	6	7	8
9	10	11	12	13	14	15
16	17	18	19	20	21	22
23	24	25	26	27	28	29
30						

October 2013

M	T	W	T	F	S	S
	1	2	3	4	5	6
7	8	9	10	11	12	13
14	15	16	17	18	19	20
21	22	23	24	25	26	27
28	29	30	31			

November 2013

M	T	W	T	F	S	S
				1	2	3
4	5	6	7	8	9	10
11	12	13	14	15	16	17
18	19	20	21	22	23	24
25	26	27	28	29	30	

December 2013

M	T	W	T	F	S	S
						1
2	3	4	5	6	7	8
9	10	11	12	13	14	15
16	17	18	19	20	21	22
23	24	25	26	27	28	29
30	31					

● = New Moon / Neumond / Nouvelle lune
☽ = First Quarter or Waxing Moon / Erstes Viertel, zunehmender Mond /
Premier quartier, lune montante
○ = Full Moon / Vollmond / Pleine lune
☾ = Last Quarter or Waning Moon / Letztes Viertel, abnehmender Mond /
Dernier quartier, lune descendante

Lunar phases noted in this calendar are presented in terms of Universal Time.
Unsere Angaben der Mondphasen beziehen sich auf die Universal Time.
Les phases lunaires que nous indiquons se basent sur le Temps Universel de Greenwich.

31
MONDAY • MONTAG • LUNDI •
LUNEDÌ • LUNES • MAANDAG

1
TUESDAY • DIENSTAG • MARDI •
MARTEDÌ • MARTES • DINSDAG

2
WEDNESDAY • MITTWOCH •
MERCREDI • MERCOLEDÌ •
MIÉRCOLES • WOENSDAG

New Year's Eve •
Silvester • Saint-Sylvestre •
Oudejaarsavond

Kwanzaa ends, *USA*
New Year's Day • Neujahr •
Nouvel An • Nieuwjaar

Berchtoldstag, *Switzerland*
Bank Holiday, *Scotland*

3

THURSDAY • DONNERSTAG •
JEUDI • GIOVEDÌ • JUEVES •
DONDERDAG

4

FRIDAY • FREITAG •
VENDREDI • VENERDÌ •
VIERNES • VRIJDAG

5

SATURDAY • SAMSTAG •
SAMEDI • SABATO •
SÁBADO • ZATERDAG

☾

6

SUNDAY • SONNTAG •
DIMANCHE • DOMENICA •
DOMINGO • ZONDAG

Epiphany • Heilige Drei Könige •
Epiphanie • Driekoningen

7
MONDAY • MONTAG • LUNDI •
LUNEDÌ • LUNES • MAANDAG

8
TUESDAY • DIENSTAG • MARDI •
MARTEDÌ • MARTES • DINSDAG

9
WEDNESDAY • MITTWOCH •
MERCREDI • MERCOLEDÌ •
MIÉRCOLES • WOENSDAG

10

THURSDAY • DONNERSTAG •
JEUDI • GIOVEDÌ • JUEVES •
DONDERDAG

11

FRIDAY • FREITAG •
VENDREDÌ • VENERDÌ •
VIERNES • VRIJDAG

12

SATURDAY • SAMSTAG •
SAMEDI • SABATO •
SÁBADO • ZATERDAG

13

SUNDAY • SONNTAG •
DIMANCHE • DOMENICA •
DOMINGO • ZONDAG

14
MONDAY • MONTAG • LUNDI •
LUNEDÌ • LUNES • MAANDAG

15
TUESDAY • DIENSTAG • MARDI •
MARTEDÌ • MARTES • DINSDAG

16
WEDNESDAY • MITTWOCH •
MERCREDI • MERCOLEDÌ •
MIÉRCOLES • WOENSDAG

17

THURSDAY • DONNERSTAG •
JEUDI • GIOVEDÌ • JUEVES •
DONDERDAG

18

FRIDAY • FREITAG •
VENDREDI • VENERDÌ •
VIERNES • VRIJDAG

☽

19

SATURDAY • SAMSTAG •
SAMEDI • SABATO •
SÁBADO • ZATERDAG

20

SUNDAY • SONNTAG •
DIMANCHE • DOMENICA •
DOMINGO • ZONDAG

21
MONDAY • MONTAG • LUNDI •
LUNEDÌ • LUNES • MAANDAG

22
TUESDAY • DIENSTAG • MARDI •
MARTEDÌ • MARTES • DINSDAG

23
WEDNESDAY • MITTWOCH •
MERCREDI • MERCOLEDÌ •
MIÉRCOLES • WOENSDAG

Martin Luther King, Jr.'s
Birthday, *USA*

24
THURSDAY • DONNERSTAG •
JEUDI • GIOVEDÌ • JUEVES •
DONDERDAG

25
FRIDAY • FREITAG •
VENDREDI • VENERDÌ •
VIERNES • VRIJDAG

26
SATURDAY • SAMSTAG •
SAMEDI • SABATO •
SÁBADO • ZATERDAG

Australia Day, *Australia*

27
SUNDAY • SONNTAG •
DIMANCHE • DOMENICA •
DOMINGO • ZONDAG

○

Robert Burns Day, *Scotland*
Tou Bichvat • Tu Bishvat
(begins at sundown)

28
MONDAY • MONTAG • LUNDI •
LUNEDÌ • LUNES • MAANDAG

29
TUESDAY • DIENSTAG • MARDI •
MARTEDÌ • MARTES • DINSDAG

30
WEDNESDAY • MITTWOCH •
MERCREDI • MERCOLEDÌ •
MIÉRCOLES • WOENSDAG

2013

31

THURSDAY • DONNERSTAG •
JEUDI • GIOVEDÌ • JUEVES •
DONDERDAG

1

FRIDAY • FREITAG •
VENDREDI • VENERDÌ •
VIERNES • VRIJDAG

2

SATURDAY • SAMSTAG •
SAMEDI • SABATO •
SÁBADO • ZATERDAG

3

SUNDAY • SONNTAG •
DIMANCHE • DOMENICA •
DOMINGO • ZONDAG

☾

Koningin Beatrix (1938),
Netherlands

5 WEEK

4
MONDAY • MONTAG • LUNDI •
LUNEDÌ • LUNES • MAANDAG

5
TUESDAY • DIENSTAG • MARDI •
MARTEDÌ • MARTES • DINSDAG

6
WEDNESDAY • MITTWOCH •
MERCREDI • MERCOLEDÌ •
MIÉRCOLES • WOENSDAG

Waitangi Day, *New Zealand*

SCARBOROUGH

BOOKLET FROM PUBLICITY DEPARTMENT, SCARBOROUGH

Train services and fares from stations, offices and agencies

British Railways poster, Scarborough, 1958-1959
© Mary Evans / The National Archives. London. England

*Those who have crossed more than once
invariably choose their ship with care*

S.S.
RELIANCE
ALBERT BALLIN

AND OTHER SPLENDID STEAMERS

S.S.
RESOLUTE
DEUTSCHLAND

UNITED AMERICAN LINES
(HARRIMAN LINE)
joint service with
HAMBURG AMERICAN LINE

Write for fascinating travel booklet P. Q.

59 BROADWAY, NEW YORK

171 W. RANDOLPH ST., CHICAGO   230 CALIFORNIA ST., SAN FRANCISCO

Boarding a ship of the United American Lines
© Mary Evans Picture Library

7

THURSDAY • DONNERSTAG •
JEUDI • GIOVEDÌ • JUEVES •
DONDERDAG

8

FRIDAY • FREITAG •
VENDREDI • VENERDÌ •
VIERNES • VRIJDAG

9

SATURDAY • SAMSTAG •
SAMEDI • SABATO •
SÁBADO • ZATERDAG

10

SUNDAY • SONNTAG •
DIMANCHE • DOMENICA •
DOMINGO • ZONDAG

●

Chinese (Lunar) New Year

11

MONDAY • MONTAG • LUNDI • LUNEDÌ • LUNES • MAANDAG

12

TUESDAY • DIENSTAG • MARDI • MARTEDÌ • MARTES • DINSDAG

13

WEDNESDAY • MITTWOCH • MERCREDI • MERCOLEDÌ • MIÉRCOLES • WOENSDAG

Rosenmontag, *Germany*

Fastnacht, *Germany*
Shrove Tuesday • Mardi Gras, *Canada, France, USA*

Ash Wednesday •
Aschermittwoch •
Cendres • Aswoensdag

14

THURSDAY • DONNERSTAG •
JEUDI • GIOVEDÌ • JUEVES •
DONDERDAG

15

FRIDAY • FREITAG •
VENDREDI • VENERDÌ •
VIERNES • VRIJDAG

16

SATURDAY • SAMSTAG •
SAMEDI • SABATO •
SÁBADO • ZATERDAG

17

SUNDAY • SONNTAG •
DIMANCHE • DOMENICA •
DOMINGO • ZONDAG

☽

St. Valentine's Day •
Valentinstag • Saint-Valentin •
Valentijnsdag

18
MONDAY • MONTAG • LUNDI •
LUNEDÌ • LUNES • MAANDAG

19
TUESDAY • DIENSTAG • MARDI •
MARTEDÌ • MARTES • DINSDAG

20
WEDNESDAY • MITTWOCH •
MERCREDI • MERCOLEDÌ •
MIÉRCOLES • WOENSDAG

Washington's Birthday
(President's Day), *USA*

21

THURSDAY • DONNERSTAG •
JEUDI • GIOVEDÌ • JUEVES •
DONDERDAG

22

FRIDAY • FREITAG •
VENDREDI • VENERDÌ •
VIERNES • VRIJDAG

23

SATURDAY • SAMSTAG •
SAMEDI • SABATO •
SÁBADO • ZATERDAG

Pourim • Purim
(begins at sundown)

24

SUNDAY • SONNTAG •
DIMANCHE • DOMENICA •
DOMINGO • ZONDAG

25

MONDAY • MONTAG • LUNDI •
LUNEDÌ • LUNES • MAANDAG

26

TUESDAY • DIENSTAG • MARDI •
MARTEDÌ • MARTES • DINSDAG

27

WEDNESDAY • MITTWOCH •
MERCREDI • MERCOLEDÌ •
MIÉRCOLES • WOENSDAG

28
THURSDAY • DONNERSTAG •
JEUDI • GIOVEDÌ • JUEVES •
DONDERDAG

1
FRIDAY • FREITAG •
VENDREDI • VENERDÌ •
VIERNES • VRIJDAG

2
SATURDAY • SAMSTAG •
SAMEDI • SABATO •
SÁBADO • ZATERDAG

3
SUNDAY • SONNTAG •
DIMANCHE • DOMENICA •
DOMINGO • ZONDAG

St. David's Day, *Wales*

4

MONDAY • MONTAG • LUNDI •
LUNEDÌ • LUNES • MAANDAG

☾

5

TUESDAY • DIENSTAG • MARDI •
MARTEDÌ • MARTES • DINSDAG

6

WEDNESDAY • MITTWOCH •
MERCREDI • MERCOLEDÌ •
MIÉRCOLES • WOENSDAG

7

THURSDAY • DONNERSTAG •
JEUDI • GIOVEDÌ • JUEVES •
DONDERDAG

8

FRIDAY • FREITAG •
VENDREDI • VENERDÌ •
VIERNES • VRIJDAG

9

SATURDAY • SAMSTAG •
SAMEDI • SABATO •
SÁBADO • ZATERDAG

10

SUNDAY • SONNTAG •
DIMANCHE • DOMENICA •
DOMINGO • ZONDAG

Daylight Saving Time begins,
Canada, USA
Mothering Sunday
(Mother's Day), *UK*

11
MONDAY • MONTAG • LUNDI •
LUNEDÌ • LUNES • MAANDAG

12
TUESDAY • DIENSTAG • MARDI •
MARTEDÌ • MARTES • DINSDAG

13
WEDNESDAY • MITTWOCH •
MERCREDI • MERCOLEDÌ •
MIÉRCOLES • WOENSDAG

14
THURSDAY • DONNERSTAG •
JEUDI • GIOVEDÌ • JUEVES •
DONDERDAG

15
FRIDAY • FREITAG •
VENDREDI • VENERDÌ •
VIERNES • VRIJDAG

16
SATURDAY • SAMSTAG •
SAMEDI • SABATO •
SÁBADO • ZATERDAG

17
SUNDAY • SONNTAG •
DIMANCHE • DOMENICA •
DOMINGO • ZONDAG

St. Patrick's Day, *N. Ireland,*
Rep. of Ireland, USA

18

MONDAY • MONTAG • LUNDI •
LUNEDÌ • LUNES • MAANDAG

19

TUESDAY • DIENSTAG • MARDI •
MARTEDÌ • MARTES • DINSDAG

☽

Josephstag, *Switzerland*

20

WEDNESDAY • MITTWOCH •
MERCREDI • MERCOLEDÌ •
MIÉRCOLES • WOENSDAG

Vernal Equinox • Frühlings-
Tagundnachtgleiche • Printemps
(11:02 Universal Time)

21
THURSDAY • DONNERSTAG •
JEUDI • GIOVEDÌ • JUEVES •
DONDERDAG

22
FRIDAY • FREITAG •
VENDREDI • VENERDÌ •
VIERNES • VRIJDAG

23
SATURDAY • SAMSTAG •
SAMEDI • SABATO •
SÁBADO • ZATERDAG

24
SUNDAY • SONNTAG •
DIMANCHE • DOMENICA •
DOMINGO • ZONDAG

Palm Sunday • Palmsonntag •
Dimanche des Rameaux •
Palmzondag

25

MONDAY • MONTAG • LUNDI •
LUNEDÌ • LUNES • MAANDAG

26

TUESDAY • DIENSTAG • MARDI •
MARTEDÌ • MARTES • DINSDAG

27

WEDNESDAY • MITTWOCH •
MERCREDI • MERCOLEDÌ •
MIÉRCOLES • WOENSDAG

○

Pessa'h • Pesach
(begins at sundown)

28

THURSDAY • DONNERSTAG •
JEUDI • GIOVEDÌ • JUEVES •
DONDERDAG

29

FRIDAY • FREITAG •
VENDREDI • VENERDÌ •
VIERNES • VRIJDAG

30

SATURDAY • SAMSTAG •
SAMEDI • SABATO •
SÁBADO • ZATERDAG

31

SUNDAY • SONNTAG •
DIMANCHE • DOMENICA •
DOMINGO • ZONDAG

Easter Sunday • Ostersonntag •
Pâques • Pasen
Clocks forward one hour, *UK*
Begin zomertijd, *Belgium,
Netherlands*
Beginn der Sommerzeit,
Austria, Germany, Switzerland

Good Friday •
Karfreitag •
Vendredi Saint •
Goede Vrijdag
Bank Holiday, *UK*

Gründonnerstag, *Germany*
Witte Donderdag, *Belgium,
Netherlands*

13 WEEK

1

MONDAY • MONTAG • LUNDI •
LUNEDÌ • LUNES • MAANDAG

2

TUESDAY • DIENSTAG • MARDI •
MARTEDÌ • MARTES • DINSDAG

3

WEDNESDAY • MITTWOCH •
MERCREDI • MERCOLEDÌ •
MIÉRCOLES • WOENSDAG

☾

Easter Monday • Ostermontag •
Lundi de Pâques • Tweede paas-
dag | Bank Holiday, UK

LAGO DI GARDA

BARABINO E GRAEVE GENOVA

Advert for the Golden Arrow cross channel sleeper train between London, Calais and Paris
© Mary Evans Picture Library/ONSLOW AUCTIONS LIMITED

4

THURSDAY • DONNERSTAG •
JEUDI • GIOVEDÌ • JUEVES •
DONDERDAG

5

FRIDAY • FREITAG •
VENDREDI • VENERDÌ •
VIERNES • VRIJDAG

6

SATURDAY • SAMSTAG •
SAMEDI • SABATO •
SÁBADO • ZATERDAG

Yom HaShoah (Holocaust
Remembrance Day – begins
at sundown)

7

SUNDAY • SONNTAG •
DIMANCHE • DOMENICA •
DOMINGO • ZONDAG

8
MONDAY • MONTAG • LUNDI •
LUNEDÌ • LUNES • MAANDAG

9
TUESDAY • DIENSTAG • MARDI •
MARTEDÌ • MARTES • DINSDAG

10
WEDNESDAY • MITTWOCH •
MERCREDI • MERCOLEDÌ •
MIÉRCOLES • WOENSDAG

2013

APRIL • ABRIL • APRILE • AVRIL • APRIL • **APRIL**

11
THURSDAY • DONNERSTAG •
JEUDI • GIOVEDÌ • JUEVES •
DONDERDAG

12
FRIDAY • FREITAG •
VENDREDI • VENERDÌ •
VIERNES • VRIJDAG

13
SATURDAY • SAMSTAG •
SAMEDI • SABATO •
SÁBADO • ZATERDAG

14
SUNDAY • SONNTAG •
DIMANCHE • DOMENICA •
DOMINGO • ZONDAG

15 WEEK

15
MONDAY • MONTAG • LUNDI •
LUNEDÌ • LUNES • MAANDAG

16
TUESDAY • DIENSTAG • MARDI •
MARTEDÌ • MARTES • DINSDAG

17
WEDNESDAY • MITTWOCH •
MERCREDI • MERCOLEDÌ •
MIÉRCOLES • WOENSDAG

Yom Ha'atzmaout •
Yom HaAtzmaut
(begins at sundown)

18

THURSDAY • DONNERSTAG •
JEUDI • GIOVEDÌ • JUEVES •
DONDERDAG

☽

19

FRIDAY • FREITAG •
VENDREDI • VENERDÌ •
VIERNES • VRIJDAG

20

SATURDAY • SAMSTAG •
SAMEDI • SABATO •
SÁBADO • ZATERDAG

21

SUNDAY • SONNTAG •
DIMANCHE • DOMENICA •
DOMINGO • ZONDAG

22

MONDAY • MONTAG • LUNDI •
LUNEDÌ • LUNES • MAANDAG

23

TUESDAY • DIENSTAG • MARDI •
MARTEDÌ • MARTES • DINSDAG

24

WEDNESDAY • MITTWOCH •
MERCREDI • MERCOLEDÌ •
MIÉRCOLES • WOENSDAG

St. George's Day, *England*

2013

APRIL • ABRIL • APRILE • AVRIL • APRIL • **APRIL**

25
THURSDAY • DONNERSTAG •
JEUDI • GIOVEDÌ • JUEVES •
DONDERDAG

○

26
FRIDAY • FREITAG •
VENDREDI • VENERDÌ •
VIERNES • VRIJDAG

27
SATURDAY • SAMSTAG •
SAMEDI • SABATO •
SÁBADO • ZATERDAG

Prins Willem Alexander (1967),
Netherlands | Lag BaOmer
(begins at sundown)

28
SUNDAY • SONNTAG •
DIMANCHE • DOMENICA •
DOMINGO • ZONDAG

*Anzac Day, Australia,
New Zealand*

17 WEEK

29

MONDAY • MONTAG • LUNDI •
LUNEDÌ • LUNES • MAANDAG

30

TUESDAY • DIENSTAG • MARDI •
MARTEDÌ • MARTES • DINSDAG

1

WEDNESDAY • MITTWOCH •
MERCREDI • MERCOLEDÌ •
MIÉRCOLES • WOENSDAG

Koninginnedag, *Netherlands*

Dag van de Arbeid, *Netherlands*
Feest van de Arbeid, *Belgium*
Fête du travail, *France*
Maifeiertag, *Germany*
Staatsfeiertag, *Austria*
Tag der Arbeit, *Switzerland*

MEI • MAYO • MAGGIO • MAI • MAI • **MAY**

2

THURSDAY • DONNERSTAG •
JEUDI • GIOVEDÌ • JUEVES •
DONDERDAG

☾

3

FRIDAY • FREITAG •
VENDREDI • VENERDÌ •
VIERNES • VRIJDAG

4

SATURDAY • SAMSTAG •
SAMEDI • SABATO •
SÁBADO • ZATERDAG

Herdenking der gevallenen,
Netherlands

5

SUNDAY • SONNTAG •
DIMANCHE • DOMENICA •
DOMINGO • ZONDAG

Bevrijdingsdag, *Netherlands*

18 WEEK

6
MONDAY • MONTAG • LUNDI •
LUNEDÌ • LUNES • MAANDAG

7
TUESDAY • DIENSTAG • MARDI •
MARTEDÌ • MARTES • DINSDAG

8
WEDNESDAY • MITTWOCH •
MERCREDI • MERCOLEDÌ •
MIÉRCOLES • WOENSDAG

May Day Bank Holiday, *UK,*
Rep. of Ireland, Australia

Fête de la Victoire 1945,
France

9

THURSDAY • DONNERSTAG •
JEUDI • GIOVEDÌ • JUEVES •
DONDERDAG

10

FRIDAY • FREITAG •
VENDREDI • VENERDÌ •
VIERNES • VRIJDAG

11

SATURDAY • SAMSTAG •
SAMEDI • SABATO •
SÁBADO • ZATERDAG

12

SUNDAY • SONNTAG •
DIMANCHE • DOMENICA •
DOMINGO • ZONDAG

Ascension Day • Christi
Himmelfahrt • Ascension •
Hemelvaartsdag • Auffahrt

Mother's Day • Muttertag •
Moederdag

13

MONDAY • MONTAG • LUNDI •
LUNEDÌ • LUNES • MAANDAG

14

TUESDAY • DIENSTAG • MARDI •
MARTEDÌ • MARTES • DINSDAG

15

WEDNESDAY • MITTWOCH •
MERCREDI • MERCOLEDÌ •
MIÉRCOLES • WOENSDAG

Chavouoth • Shavuot
(begins at sundown)

2013

16
THURSDAY • DONNERSTAG •
JEUDI • GIOVEDÌ • JUEVES •
DONDERDAG

17
FRIDAY • FREITAG •
VENDREDI • VENERDÌ •
VIERNES • VRIJDAG

18
SATURDAY • SAMSTAG •
SAMEDI • SABATO •
SÁBADO • ZATERDAG

☽

19
SUNDAY • SONNTAG •
DIMANCHE • DOMENICA •
DOMINGO • ZONDAG

Pentecost Sunday •
Pfingstsonntag •
Pentecôte • Pinksteren

20

MONDAY • MONTAG • LUNDI •
LUNEDÌ • LUNES • MAANDAG

21

TUESDAY • DIENSTAG • MARDI •
MARTEDÌ • MARTES • DINSDAG

22

WEDNESDAY • MITTWOCH •
MERCREDI • MERCOLEDÌ •
MIÉRCOLES • WOENSDAG

Pentecost Monday • Pfingst-
montag • Lundi de Pentecôte •
Tweede pinksterdag
Victoria Day, *Canada*

23

THURSDAY • DONNERSTAG •
JEUDI • GIOVEDÌ • JUEVES •
DONDERDAG

24

FRIDAY • FREITAG •
VENDREDI • VENERDÌ •
VIERNES • VRIJDAG

25

SATURDAY • SAMSTAG •
SAMEDI • SABATO •
SÁBADO • ZATERDAG

○

26

SUNDAY • SONNTAG •
DIMANCHE • DOMENICA •
DOMINGO • ZONDAG

Fête des Mères, *France*

27

MONDAY • MONTAG • LUNDI •
LUNEDÌ • LUNES • MAANDAG

28

TUESDAY • DIENSTAG • MARDI •
MARTEDÌ • MARTES • DINSDAG

29

WEDNESDAY • MITTWOCH •
MERCREDI • MERCOLEDÌ •
MIÉRCOLES • WOENSDAG

Memorial Day, *USA*
Spring Bank Holiday, *UK*

30
THURSDAY • DONNERSTAG •
JEUDI • GIOVEDÌ • JUEVES •
DONDERDAG

31
FRIDAY • FREITAG •
VENDREDI • VENERDÌ •
VIERNES • VRIJDAG

☾

1
SATURDAY • SAMSTAG •
SAMEDI • SABATO •
SÁBADO • ZATERDAG

2
SUNDAY • SONNTAG •
DIMANCHE • DOMENICA •
DOMINGO • ZONDAG

Fronleichnam, *Austria, Germany,
Switzerland*

3
MONDAY • MONTAG • LUNDI •
LUNEDÌ • LUNES • MAANDAG

4
TUESDAY • DIENSTAG • MARDI •
MARTEDÌ • MARTES • DINSDAG

5
WEDNESDAY • MITTWOCH •
MERCREDI • MERCOLEDÌ •
MIÉRCOLES • WOENSDAG

Queen's Birthday, *New Zealand*
Bank Holiday, *Rep. of Ireland*

6

THURSDAY • DONNERSTAG •
JEUDI • GIOVEDÌ • JUEVES •
DONDERDAG

7

FRIDAY • FREITAG •
VENDREDI • VENERDÌ •
VIERNES • VRIJDAG

8

SATURDAY • SAMSTAG •
SAMEDI • SABATO •
SÁBADO • ZATERDAG
●

9

SUNDAY • SONNTAG •
DIMANCHE • DOMENICA •
DOMINGO • ZONDAG

10
MONDAY • MONTAG • LUNDI •
LUNEDÌ • LUNES • MAANDAG

11
TUESDAY • DIENSTAG • MARDI •
MARTEDÌ • MARTES • DINSDAG

12
WEDNESDAY • MITTWOCH •
MERCREDI • MERCOLEDÌ •
MIÉRCOLES • WOENSDAG

13
THURSDAY • DONNERSTAG •
JEUDI • GIOVEDÌ • JUEVES •
DONDERDAG

14
FRIDAY • FREITAG •
VENDREDI • VENERDÌ •
VIERNES • VRIJDAG

15
SATURDAY • SAMSTAG •
SAMEDI • SABATO •
SÁBADO • ZATERDAG

16
SUNDAY • SONNTAG •
DIMANCHE • DOMENICA •
DOMINGO • ZONDAG

☽

Father's Day • Fête des Pères •
Vaderdag

17
MONDAY • MONTAG • LUNDI •
LUNEDÌ • LUNES • MAANDAG

18
TUESDAY • DIENSTAG • MARDI •
MARTEDÌ • MARTES • DINSDAG

19
WEDNESDAY • MITTWOCH •
MERCREDI • MERCOLEDÌ •
MIÉRCOLES • WOENSDAG

20

THURSDAY • DONNERSTAG •
JEUDI • GIOVEDÌ • JUEVES •
DONDERDAG

21

FRIDAY • FREITAG •
VENDREDI • VENERDÌ •
VIERNES • VRIJDAG

22

SATURDAY • SAMSTAG •
SAMEDI • SABATO •
SÁBADO • ZATERDAG

23

SUNDAY • SONNTAG •
DIMANCHE • DOMENICA •
DOMINGO • ZONDAG

○

Summer Solstice • Sommer-
sonnenwende • Solstice d'été
(05:04 Universal Time)

24

MONDAY • MONTAG • LUNDI •
LUNEDÌ • LUNES • MAANDAG

25

TUESDAY • DIENSTAG • MARDI •
MARTEDÌ • MARTES • DINSDAG

26

WEDNESDAY • MITTWOCH •
MERCREDI • MERCOLEDÌ •
MIÉRCOLES • WOENSDAG

St. Jean Baptiste Day,
Canada (Quebec)

27
THURSDAY • DONNERSTAG •
JEUDI • GIOVEDÌ • JUEVES •
DONDERDAG

28
FRIDAY • FREITAG •
VENDREDI • VENERDÌ •
VIERNES • VRIJDAG

29
SATURDAY • SAMSTAG •
SAMEDI • SABATO •
SÁBADO • ZATERDAG

30
SUNDAY • SONNTAG •
DIMANCHE • DOMENICA •
DOMINGO • ZONDAG

☾

1
MONDAY • MONTAG • LUNDI •
LUNEDÌ • LUNES • MAANDAG

2
TUESDAY • DIENSTAG • MARDI •
MARTEDÌ • MARTES • DINSDAG

3
WEDNESDAY • MITTWOCH •
MERCREDI • MERCOLEDÌ •
MIÉRCOLES • WOENSDAG

Canada Day, *Canada*

4

THURSDAY • DONNERSTAG •
JEUDI • GIOVEDÌ • JUEVES •
DONDERDAG

5

FRIDAY • FREITAG •
VENDREDI • VENERDÌ •
VIERNES • VRIJDAG

6

SATURDAY • SAMSTAG •
SAMEDI • SABATO •
SÁBADO • ZATERDAG

7

SUNDAY • SONNTAG •
DIMANCHE • DOMENICA •
DOMINGO • ZONDAG

Independence Day, *USA*

8
MONDAY • MONTAG • LUNDI •
LUNEDÍ • LUNES • MAANDAG

9
TUESDAY • DIENSTAG • MARDI •
MARTEDÍ • MARTES • DINSDAG

10
WEDNESDAY • MITTWOCH •
MERCREDI • MERCOLEDÍ •
MIÉRCOLES • WOENSDAG

11

THURSDAY • DONNERSTAG •
JEUDI • GIOVEDÌ • JUEVES •
DONDERDAG

12

FRIDAY • FREITAG •
VENDREDI • VENERDÌ •
VIERNES • VRIJDAG

13

SATURDAY • SAMSTAG •
SAMEDI • SABATO •
SÁBADO • ZATERDAG

14

SUNDAY • SONNTAG •
DIMANCHE • DOMENICA •
DOMINGO • ZONDAG

Battle of the Boyne
(Orangemen's Day), *N. Ireland*

Fête Nationale, *France*

15
MONDAY • MONTAG • LUNDI •
LUNEDÌ • LUNES • MAANDAG

16
TUESDAY • DIENSTAG • MARDI •
MARTEDÌ • MARTES • DINSDAG

☽

17
WEDNESDAY • MITTWOCH •
MERCREDI • MERCOLEDÌ •
MIÉRCOLES • WOENSDAG

Tisha Beav • Tisha B'Av
(begins at sundown)

18

THURSDAY • DONNERSTAG •
JEUDI • GIOVEDÌ • JUEVES •
DONDERDAG

19

FRIDAY • FREITAG •
VENDREDI • VENERDÌ •
VIERNES • VRIJDAG

20

SATURDAY • SAMSTAG •
SAMEDI • SÁBATO •
SÁBADO • ZATERDAG

21

SUNDAY • SONNTAG •
DIMANCHE • DOMENICA •
DOMINGO • ZONDAG

Nationale Feestdag /
Fête Nationale, *Belgium*

22

MONDAY • MONTAG • LUNDI •
LUNEDÌ • LUNES • MAANDAG

○

23

TUESDAY • DIENSTAG • MARDI •
MARTEDÌ • MARTES • DINSDAG

24

WEDNESDAY • MITTWOCH •
MERCREDI • MERCOLEDÌ •
MIÉRCOLES • WOENSDAG

Poster advertising Illovo Beach, a small coastal resort in Natal, South Africa.
© Mary Evans Picture Library/ONSLOW AUCTIONS LIMITED

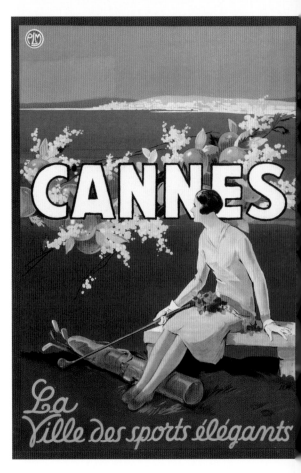

Poster advertising Cannes, the town of elegant sports (not to mention the famous film festival).
A well to do lady sits on a bench, no doubt resting from her golfing exertions.
© Mary Evans Picture Library/ONSLOW AUCTIONS LIMITED

25
THURSDAY • DONNERSTAG •
JEUDI • GIOVEDÌ • JUEVES •
DONDERDAG

26
FRIDAY • FREITAG •
VENDREDI • VENERDÌ •
VIERNES • VRIJDAG

27
SATURDAY • SAMSTAG •
SAMEDI • SABATO •
SÁBADO • ZATERDAG

28
SUNDAY • SONNTAG •
DIMANCHE • DOMENICA •
DOMINGO • ZONDAG

29
MONDAY • MONTAG • LUNDI •
LUNEDÌ • LUNES • MAANDAG

☾

30
TUESDAY • DIENSTAG • MARDI •
MARTEDÌ • MARTES • DINSDAG

31
WEDNESDAY • MITTWOCH •
MERCREDI • MERCOLEDÌ •
MIÉRCOLES • WOENSDAG

1

THURSDAY • DONNERSTAG •
JEUDI • GIOVEDÌ • JUEVES •
DONDERDAG

2

FRIDAY • FREITAG •
VENDREDI • VENERDÌ •
VIERNES • VRIJDAG

3

SATURDAY • SAMSTAG •
SAMEDI • SABATO •
SÁBADO • ZATERDAG

4

SUNDAY • SONNTAG •
DIMANCHE • DOMENICA •
DOMINGO • ZONDAG

Nationalfeiertag, *Switzerland*

31 WEEK

5
MONDAY • MONTAG • LUNDI •
LUNEDÌ • LUNES • MAANDAG

6
TUESDAY • DIENSTAG • MARDI •
MARTEDÌ • MARTES • DINSDAG

7
WEDNESDAY • MITTWOCH •
MERCREDI • MERCOLEDÌ •
MIÉRCOLES • WOENSDAG

Summer Bank Holiday,
Rep. of Ireland, Scotland

8

THURSDAY • DONNERSTAG •
JEUDI • GIOVEDÌ • JUEVES •
DONDERDAG

9

FRIDAY • FREITAG •
VENDREDI • VENERDÌ •
VIERNES • VRIJDAG

10

SATURDAY • SAMSTAG •
SAMEDI • SABATO •
SÁBADO • ZATERDAG

11

SUNDAY • SONNTAG •
DIMANCHE • DOMENICA •
DOMINGO • ZONDAG

12

MONDAY • MONTAG • LUNDI •
LUNEDÌ • LUNES • MAANDAG

13

TUESDAY • DIENSTAG • MARDI •
MARTEDÌ • MARTES • DINSDAG

14

WEDNÉSDAY • MITTWOCH •
MERCREDI • MERCOLEDÌ •
MIÉRCOLES • WOENSDAG

☽

15

THURSDAY • DONNERSTAG •
JEUDI • GIOVEDÌ • JUEVES •
DONDERDAG

16

FRIDAY • FREITAG •
VENDREDI • VENERDÌ •
VIERNES • VRIJDAG

17

SATURDAY • SAMSTAG •
SAMEDI • SABATO •
SÁBADO • ZATERDAG

18

SUNDAY • SONNTAG •
DIMANCHE • DOMENICA •
DOMINGO • ZONDAG

Feast of the Assumption •
Mariä Himmelfahrt •
Assomption •
Maria-Tenhemelopneming

19
MONDAY • MONTAG • LUNDI •
LUNEDÌ • LUNES • MAANDAG

20
TUESDAY • DIENSTAG • MARDI •
MARTEDÌ • MARTES • DINSDAG

21
WEDNESDAY • MITTWOCH •
MERCREDI • MERCOLEDÌ •
MIÉRCOLES • WOENSDAG
○

22
THURSDAY • DONNERSTAG •
JEUDI • GIOVEDÌ • JUEVES •
DONDERDAG

23
FRIDAY • FREITAG •
VENDREDI • VENERDÌ •
VIERNES • VRIJDAG

24
SATURDAY • SAMSTAG •
SAMEDI • SABATO •
SÁBADO • ZATERDAG

25
SUNDAY • SONNTAG •
DIMANCHE • DOMENICA •
DOMINGO • ZONDAG

26
MONDAY • MONTAG • LUNDI •
LUNEDÌ • LUNES • MAANDAG

27
TUESDAY • DIENSTAG • MARDI •
MARTEDÌ • MARTES • DINSDAG

28
WEDNESDAY • MITTWOCH •
MERCREDI • MERCOLEDÌ •
MIÉRCOLES • WOENSDAG

☾

Summer Bank Holiday, *UK*
(except *Scotland*)

2013

AUGUSTUS • AGOSTO • AGOSTO • AOÛT • AUGUST • **AUGUST**
SEPTEMBER • SEPTIEMBRE • SETTEMBRE • SEPTEMBRE • SEPTEMBER • **SEPTEMBER**

29

THURSDAY • DONNERSTAG •
JEUDI • GIOVEDÌ • JUEVES •
DONDERDAG

30

FRIDAY • FREITAG •
VENDREDI • VENERDÌ •
VIERNES • VRIJDAG

31

SATURDAY • SAMSTAG •
SAMEDI • SABATO •
SÁBADO • ZATERDAG

1

SUNDAY • SONNTAG •
DIMANCHE • DOMENICA •
DOMINGO • ZONDAG

35 WEEK

2

MONDAY • MONTAG • LUNDI •
LUNEDÌ • LUNES • MAANDAG

3

TUESDAY • DIENSTAG • MARDI •
MARTEDÌ • MARTES • DINSDAG

4

WEDNESDAY • MITTWOCH •
MERCREDI • MERCOLEDÌ •
MIÉRCOLES • WOENSDAG

Labor Day, *USA*
Labour Day, *Canada*

Roch Hachana • Rosh HaShana
(begins at sundown)

5

THURSDAY • DONNERSTAG •
JEUDI • GIOVEDÌ • JUEVES •
DONDERDAG

6

FRIDAY • FREITAG •
VENDREDI • VENERDÌ •
VIERNES • VRIJDAG

7

SATURDAY • SAMSTAG •
SAMEDI • SABATO •
SÁBADO • ZATERDAG

8

SUNDAY • SONNTAG •
DIMANCHE • DOMENICA •
DOMINGO • ZONDAG

9
MONDAY • MONTAG • LUNDI •
LUNEDÌ • LUNES • MAANDAG

10
TUESDAY • DIENSTAG • MARDI •
MARTEDÌ • MARTES • DINSDAG

11
WEDNESDAY • MITTWOCH •
MERCREDI • MERCOLEDÌ •
MIÉRCOLES • WOENSDAG

12

THURSDAY • DONNERSTAG •
JEUDI • GIOVEDÌ • JUEVES •
DONDERDAG

☽

13

FRIDAY • FREITAG •
VENDREDI • VENERDÌ •
VIERNES • VRIJDAG

14

SATURDAY • SAMSTAG •
SAMEDI • SABATO •
SÁBADO • ZATERDAG

15

SUNDAY • SONNTAG •
DIMANCHE • DOMENICA •
DOMINGO • ZONDAG

Yom Kippour • Yom Kippur
(begins at sundown)

Eidgenössischer Dank-,
Buß- und Bettag, *Switzerland*

16
MONDAY • MONTAG • LUNDI •
LUNEDÌ • LUNES • MAANDAG

17
TUESDAY • DIENSTAG • MARDI •
MARTEDÌ • MARTES • DINSDAG

18
WEDNESDAY • MITTWOCH •
MERCREDI • MERCOLEDÌ •
MIÉRCOLES • WOENSDAG

Souccot • Sukkot
(begins at sundown)

By P&O to Australia via Egypt and Ceylon
© Mary Evans Picture Library

Poster inviting you to go winter-sporting at Mont-Revard, in the French Alps
© Mary Evans Picture Library

19

THURSDAY • DONNERSTAG •
JEUDI • GIOVEDÌ • JUEVES •
DONDERDAG

○

20

FRIDAY • FREITAG •
VENDREDI • VENERDÌ •
VIERNES • VRIJDAG

21

SATURDAY • SAMSTAG •
SAMEDI • SABATO •
SÁBADO • ZATERDAG

U.N. International Day of Peace

22

SUNDAY • SONNTAG •
DIMANCHE • DOMENICA •
DOMINGO • ZONDAG

Autumnal Equinox • Herbst-
Tagundnachtgleiche • Automne
(20:44 Universal Time)

23
MONDAY • MONTAG • LUNDI •
LUNEDÌ • LUNES • MAANDAG

24
TUESDAY • DIENSTAG • MARDI •
MARTEDÌ • MARTES • DINSDAG

25
WEDNESDAY • MITTWOCH •
MERCREDI • MERCOLEDÌ •
MIÉRCOLES • WOENSDAG

Chemini Atseret • Shmini Atzeret
(begins at sundown)

26

THURSDAY • DONNERSTAG •
JEUDI • GIOVEDÌ • JUEVES •
DONDERDAG

27

FRIDAY • FREITAG •
VENDREDÌ • VENERDÌ •
VIERNES • VRIJDAG

☾

28

SATURDAY • SAMSTAG •
SAMEDI • SABATO •
SÁBADO • ZATERDAG

29

SUNDAY • SONNTAG •
DIMANCHE • DOMENICA •
DOMINGO • ZONDAG

Sim'hat Torah • Simchat Torah
(begins at sundown)

30

MONDAY • MONTAG • LUNDI •
LUNEDÌ • LUNES • MAANDAG

1

TUESDAY • DIENSTAG • MARDI •
MARTEDÌ • MARTES • DINSDAG

2

WEDNESDAY • MITTWOCH •
MERCREDI • MERCOLEDÌ •
MIÉRCOLES • WOENSDAG

3

THURSDAY • DONNERSTAG •
JEUDI • GIOVEDÌ • JUEVES •
DONDERDAG

4

FRIDAY • FREITAG •
VENDREDI • VENERDÌ •
VIERNES • VRIJDAG

5

SATURDAY • SAMSTAG •
SAMEDI • SABATO •
SÁBADO • ZATERDAG

●

6

SUNDAY • SONNTAG •
DIMANCHE • DOMENICA •
DOMINGO • ZONDAG

Tag der Deutschen Einheit,
Germany

Erntedankfest, *Germany*

7
MONDAY • MONTAG • LUNDI •
LUNEDÌ • LUNES • MAANDAG

8
TUESDAY • DIENSTAG • MARDI •
MARTEDÌ • MARTES • DINSDAG

9
WEDNESDAY • MITTWOCH •
MERCREDI • MERCOLEDÌ •
MIÉRCOLES • WOENSDAG

10

THURSDAY • DONNERSTAG •
JEUDI • GIOVEDÌ • JUEVES •
DONDERDAG

11

FRIDAY • FREITAG •
VENDREDI • VENERDÌ •
VIERNES • VRIJDAG

☽

12

SATURDAY • SAMSTAG •
SAMEDI • SABATO •
SÁBADO • ZATERDAG

13

SUNDAY • SONNTAG •
DIMANCHE • DOMENICA •
DOMINGO • ZONDAG

14
MONDAY • MONTAG • LUNDI •
LUNEDİ • LUNES • MAANDAG

15
TUESDAY • DIENSTAG • MARDI •
MARTEDİ • MARTES • DINSDAG

16
WEDNESDAY • MITTWOCH •
MERCREDI • MERCOLEDİ •
MIÉRCOLES • WOENSDAG

Columbus Day, *USA*
Thanksgiving Day, *Canada*

17

THURSDAY • DONNERSTAG •
JEUDI • GIOVEDÌ • JUEVES •
DONDERDAG

18

FRIDAY • FREITAG •
VENDREDI • VENERDÌ •
VIERNES • VRIJDAG

19

SATURDAY • SAMSTAG •
SAMEDI • SABATO •
SÁBADO • ZATERDAG

20

SUNDAY • SONNTAG •
DIMANCHE • DOMENICA •
DOMINGO • ZONDAG

21

MONDAY • MONTAG • LUNDI •
LUNEDÌ • LUNES • MAANDAG

22

TUESDAY • DIENSTAG • MARDI •
MARTEDÌ • MARTES • DINSDAG

23

WEDNESDAY • MITTWOCH •
MERCREDI • MERCOLEDÌ •
MIÉRCOLES • WOENSDAG

24
THURSDAY • DONNERSTAG •
JEUDI • GIOVEDÌ • JUEVES •
DONDERDAG

25
FRIDAY • FREITAG •
VENDREDI • VENERDÌ •
VIERNES • VRIJDAG

26
SATURDAY • SAMSTAG •
SAMEDI • SABATO •
SÁBADO • ZATERDAG

☾

Nationalfeiertag, *Austria*

27
SUNDAY • SONNTAG •
DIMANCHE • DOMENICA •
DOMINGO • ZONDAG

Clocks back one hour, *UK*
Einde zomertijd, *Belgium,
Netherlands*
Ende der Sommerzeit, *Austria,
Germany, Switzerland*

28
MONDAY • MONTAG • LUNDI •
LUNEDÌ • LUNES • MAANDAG

29
TUESDAY • DIENSTAG • MARDI •
MARTEDÌ • MARTES • DINSDAG

30
WEDNESDAY • MITTWOCH •
MERCREDI • MERCOLEDÌ •
MIÉRCOLES • WOENSDAG

Bank Holiday, *Rep. of Ireland*
Labour Day, *New Zealand*

31

THURSDAY • DONNERSTAG •
JEUDI • GIOVEDÌ • JUEVES •
DONDERDAG

1

FRIDAY • FREITAG •
VENDREDI • VENERDÌ •
VIERNES • VRIJDAG

2

SATURDAY • SAMSTAG •
SAMEDI • SABATO •
SÁBADO • ZATERDAG

Allerseelen, *Austria*
Allerzielen, *Belgium,*
Netherlands

3

SUNDAY • SONNTAG •
DIMANCHE • DOMENICA •
DOMINGO • ZONDAG

●

Reformationstag, *Germany*
Halloween, *USA, UK*

All Saints' Day •
Allerheiligen • Toussaint

Daylight Saving Time ends,
USA, Canada

44 WEEK

4

MONDAY • MONTAG • LUNDI •
LUNEDÌ • LUNES • MAANDAG

5

TUESDAY • DIENSTAG • MARDI •
MARTEDÌ • MARTES • DINSDAG

6

WEDNESDAY • MITTWOCH •
MERCREDI • MERCOLEDÌ •
MIÉRCOLES • WOENSDAG

Election Day, *USA*

7

THURSDAY • DONNERSTAG •
JEUDI • GIOVEDÌ • JUEVES •
DONDERDAG

8

FRIDAY • FREITAG •
VENDREDI • VENERDÌ •
VIERNES • VRIJDAG

9

SATURDAY • SAMSTAG •
SAMEDI • SABATO •
SÁBADO • ZATERDAG

10

SUNDAY • SONNTAG •
DIMANCHE • DOMENICA •
DOMINGO • ZONDAG

☽

Remembrance Sunday, UK

11

MONDAY • MONTAG • LUNDI •
LUNEDÌ • LUNES • MAANDAG

12

TUESDAY • DIENSTAG • MARDI •
MARTEDÌ • MARTES • DINSDAG

13

WEDNESDAY • MITTWOCH •
MERCREDI • MERCOLEDÌ •
MIÉRCOLES • WOENSDAG

Martinstag, *Germany*
Armistice de 1918
(Jour du Souvenir), *France*
Remembrance Day, *Canada,
Australia*
Veteran's Day, *USA*
Wapenstilstand 1918,
Belgium

14

THURSDAY • DONNERSTAG •
JEUDI • GIOVEDÌ • JUEVES •
DONDERDAG

15

FRIDAY • FREITAG •
VENDREDI • VENERDÌ •
VIERNES • VRIJDAG

16

SATURDAY • SAMSTAG •
SAMEDI • SABATO •
SÁBADO • ZATERDAG

17

SUNDAY • SONNTAG •
DIMANCHE • DOMENICA •
DOMINGO • ZONDAG

○

Volkstrauertag, *Germany*

18

MONDAY • MONTAG • LUNDI •
LUNEDÌ • LUNES • MAANDAG

19

TUESDAY • DIENSTAG • MARDI •
MARTEDÌ • MARTES • DINSDAG

20

WEDNESDAY • MITTWOCH •
MERCREDI • MERCOLEDÌ •
MIÉRCOLES • WOENSDAG

Buß- und Bettag, *Germany*

21
THURSDAY • DONNERSTAG •
JEUDI • GIOVEDÌ • JUEVES •
DONDERDAG

22
FRIDAY • FREITAG •
VENDREDI • VENERDÌ •
VIERNES • VRIJDAG

23
SATURDAY • SAMSTAG •
SAMEDI • SABATO •
SÁBADO • ZATERDAG

24
SUNDAY • SONNTAG •
DIMANCHE • DOMENICA •
DOMINGO • ZONDAG

Totensonntag, *Germany*
Ewigkeitssonntag, *Austria*

25

MONDAY • MONTAG • LUNDI •
LUNEDÌ • LUNES • MAANDAG

☾

26

TUESDAY • DIENSTAG • MARDI •
MARTEDÌ • MARTES • DINSDAG

27

WEDNESDAY • MITTWOCH •
MERCREDI • MERCOLEDÌ •
MIÉRCOLES • WOENSDAG

Hanoucca • Chanukkah
(begins at sundown)

28

THURSDAY • DONNERSTAG •
JEUDI • GIOVEDÌ • JUEVES •
DONDERDAG

29

FRIDAY • FREITAG •
VENDREDI • VENERDÌ •
VIERNES • VRIJDAG

30

SATURDAY • SAMSTAG •
SAMEDI • SABATO •
SÁBADO • ZATERDAG

St. Andrew's Day, *Scotland*

1

SUNDAY • SONNTAG •
DIMANCHE • DOMENICA •
DOMINGO • ZONDAG

Thanksgiving Day, *USA*

2

MONDAY • MONTAG • LUNDI •
LUNEDÌ • LUNES • MAANDAG

3

TUESDAY • DIENSTAG • MARDI •
MARTEDÌ • MARTES • DINSDAG

4

WEDNESDAY • MITTWOCH •
MERCREDI • MERCOLEDÌ •
MIÉRCOLES • WOENSDAG

Bank Holiday, *Scotland*

5

THURSDAY • DONNERSTAG •
JEUDI • GIOVEDÌ • JUEVES •
DONDERDAG

6

FRIDAY • FREITAG •
VENDREDI • VENERDÌ •
VIERNES • VRIJDAG

7

SATURDAY • SAMSTAG •
SAMEDI • SABATO •
SÁBADO • ZATERDAG

8

SUNDAY • SONNTAG •
DIMANCHE • DOMENICA •
DOMINGO • ZONDAG

Sinterklaasavond, *Netherlands*

Saint-Nicolas, *France*
Sinterklaas, *Belgium,
Netherlands*

Immaculate Conception •
Mariä Empfängnis •
Immaculée Conception •
Maria-Onbevlekte-
Ontvangenis

9

MONDAY • MONTAG • LUNDI •
LUNEDÌ • LUNES • MAANDAG

☽

10

TUESDAY • DIENSTAG • MARDI •
MARTEDÌ • MARTES • DINSDAG

11

WEDNESDAY • MITTWOCH •
MERCREDI • MERCOLEDÌ •
MIÉRCOLES • WOENSDAG

12
THURSDAY • DONNERSTAG •
JEUDI • GIOVEDÌ • JUEVES •
DONDERDAG

13
FRIDAY • FREITAG •
VENDREDI • VENERDÌ •
VIERNES • VRIJDAG

14
SATURDAY • SAMSTAG •
SAMEDI • SABATO •
SÁBADO • ZATERDAG

15
SUNDAY • SONNTAG •
DIMANCHE • DOMENICA •
DOMINGO • ZONDAG

16

MONDAY • MONTAG • LUNDI •
LUNEDÌ • LUNES • MAANDAG

17

TUESDAY • DIENSTAG • MARDI •
MARTEDÌ • MARTES • DINSDAG

○

18

WEDNESDAY • MITTWOCH •
MERCREDI • MERCOLEDÌ •
MIÉRCOLES • WOENSDAG

19

THURSDAY • DONNERSTAG •
JEUDI • GIOVEDÌ • JUEVES •
DONDERDAG

20

FRIDAY • FREITAG •
VENDREDI • VENERDÌ •
VIERNES • VRIJDAG

21

SATURDAY • SAMSTAG •
SAMEDI • SABATO •
SÁBADO • ZATERDAG

Winter Solstice • Wintersonnen-
wende • Solstice d'hiver
(17:11 Universal Time)

22

SUNDAY • SONNTAG •
DIMANCHE • DOMENICA •
DOMINGO • ZONDAG

23
MONDAY • MONTAG • LUNDI •
LUNEDÌ • LUNES • MAANDAG

24
TUESDAY • DIENSTAG • MARDI •
MARTEDÌ • MARTES • DINSDAG

25
WEDNESDAY • MITTWOCH •
MERCREDI • MERCOLEDÌ •
MIÉRCOLES • WOENSDAG

☾

Christmas Eve • Heiligabend •
Veille de Noël • Kerstavond

Christmas Day • 1. Weihnachtstag •
Noël • Kerstmis
Bank Holiday, *UK*

26

THURSDAY • DONNERSTAG •
JEUDI • GIOVEDÌ • JUEVES •
DONDERDAG

27

FRIDAY • FREITAG •
VENDREDI • VENERDÌ •
VIERNES • VRIJDAG

28

SATURDAY • SAMSTAG •
SAMEDI • SABATO •
SÁBADO • ZATERDAG

29

SUNDAY • SONNTAG •
DIMANCHE • DOMENICA •
DOMINGO • ZONDAG

Boxing Day, *Australia,*
Canada, New Zealand, UK
Kwanzaa begins, *USA*
St. Stephen's Day •
Stephanitag •
Stephanstag •
2. Weihnachtstag •
Tweede kerstdag
Bank Holiday, *UK*

30

MONDAY • MONTAG • LUNDI •
LUNEDÌ • LUNES • MAANDAG

31

TUESDAY • DIENSTAG • MARDI •
MARTEDÌ • MARTES • DINSDAG

1

WEDNESDAY • MITTWOCH •
MERCREDI • MERCOLEDÌ •
MIÉRCOLES • WOENSDAG
●

New Year's Eve •
Silvester • Saint-Sylvestre •
Oudejaarsavond

Kwanzaa ends, *USA*
New Year's Day • Neujahr •
Nouvel An • Nieuwjaar
Bank Holiday, *UK*

2
THURSDAY • DONNERSTAG •
JEUDI • GIOVEDÌ • JUEVES •
DONDERDAG

3
FRIDAY • FREITAG •
VENDREDI • VENERDÌ •
VIERNES • VRIJDAG

4
SATURDAY • SAMSTAG •
SAMEDI • SABATO •
SÁBADO • ZATERDAG

5
SUNDAY • SONNTAG •
DIMANCHE • DOMENICA •
DOMINGO • ZONDAG

Berchtoldstag, *Switzerland*
Bank Holiday, *Scotland*

1	Wed	Week 1
2	Thu	
3	Fri	
4	Sat	
5	Sun	
6	Mon	Week 2
7	Tue	
8	Wed	
9	Thu	
10	Fri	
11	Sat	
12	Sun	
13	Mon	Week 3
14	Tue	
15	Wed	
16	Thu	
17	Fri	
18	Sat	
19	Sun	
20	Mon	Week 4
21	Tue	
22	Wed	
23	Thu	
24	Fri	
25	Sat	
26	Sun	
27	Mon	Week 5
28	Tue	
29	Wed	
30	Thu	
31	Fri	

1	Sat	
2	Sun	
3	Mon	Week 6
4	Tue	
5	Wed	
6	Thu	
7	Fri	
8	Sat	
9	Sun	
10	Mon	Week 7
11	Tue	
12	Wed	
13	Thu	
14	Fri	
15	Sat	
16	Sun	
17	Mon	Week 8
18	Tue	
19	Wed	
20	Thu	
21	Fri	
22	Sat	
23	Sun	
24	Mon	Week 9
25	Tue	
26	Wed	
27	Thu	
28	Fri	

1	Sat	
2	Sun	
3	Mon	Week 10
4	Tue	
5	Wed	
6	Thu	
7	Fri	
8	Sat	
9	Sun	
10	Mon	Week 11
11	Tue	
12	Wed	
13	Thu	
14	Fri	
15	Sat	
16	Sun	
17	Mon	Week 12
18	Tue	
19	Wed	
20	Thu	
21	Fri	
22	Sat	
23	Sun	
24	Mon	Week 13
25	Tue	
26	Wed	
27	Thu	
28	Fri	
29	Sat	
30	Sun	
31	Mon	Week 14

1   Tue

2   Wed

3   Thu

4   Fri

5   Sat

6   Sun

7   Mon   Week 15

8   Tue

9   Wed

10   Thu

11   Fri

12   Sat

13   Sun

14   Mon   Week 16

15   Tue

16   Wed

17   Thu

18   Fri

19   Sat

20   Sun

21   Mon   Week 17

22   Tue

23   Wed

24   Thu

25   Fri

26   Sat

27   Sun

28   Mon   Week 18

29   Tue

30   Wed

1	Thu	
2	Fri	
3	Sat	
4	Sun	
5	Mon	Week 19
6	Tue	
7	Wed	
8	Thu	
9	Fri	
10	Sat	
11	Sun	
12	Mon	Week 20
13	Tue	
14	Wed	
15	Thu	
16	Fri	
17	Sat	
18	Sun	
19	Mon	Week 21
20	Tue	
21	Wed	
22	Thu	
23	Fri	
24	Sat	
25	Sun	
26	Mon	Week 22
27	Tue	
28	Wed	
29	Thu	
30	Fri	
31	Sat	

1	Sun	
2	Mon	Week 23
3	Tue	
4	Wed	
5	Thu	
6	Fri	
7	Sat	
8	Sun	
9	Mon	Week 24
10	Tue	
11	Wed	
12	Thu	
13	Fri	
14	Sat	
15	Sun	
16	Mon	Week 25
17	Tue	
18	Wed	
19	Thu	
20	Fri	
21	Sat	
22	Sun	
23	Mon	Week 26
24	Tue	
25	Wed	
26	Thu	
27	Fri	
28	Sat	
29	Sun	
30	Mon	Week 27

1	Tue	
2	Wed	
3	Thu	
4	Fri	
5	Sat	
6	Sun	
7	Mon	Week 28
8	Tue	
9	Wed	
10	Thu	
11	Fri	
12	Sat	
13	Sun	
14	Mon	Week 29
15	Tue	
16	Wed	
17	Thu	
18	Fri	
19	Sat	
20	Sun	
21	Mon	Week 30
22	Tue	
23	Wed	
24	Thu	
25	Fri	
26	Sat	
27	Sun	
28	Mon	Week 31
29	Tue	
30	Wed	
31	Thu	

2014   **AUGUSTUS**   **AGOSTO**   **AGOSTO**   **AOÛT**   **AUGUST**   **AUGUST**

1	Fri	
2	Sat	
3	Sun	
4	Mon	Week 32
5	Tue	
6	Wed	
7	Thu	
8	Fri	
9	Sat	
10	Sun	
11	Mon	Week 33
12	Tue	
13	Wed	
14	Thu	
15	Fri	
16	Sat	
17	Sun	
18	Mon	Week 34
19	Tue	
20	Wed	
21	Thu	
22	Fri	
23	Sat	
24	Sun	
25	Mon	Week 35
26	Tue	
27	Wed	
28	Thu	
29	Fri	
30	Sat	
31	Sun	

1	Mon	Week 36
2	Tue	
3	Wed	
4	Thu	
5	Fri	
6	Sat	
7	Sun	
8	Mon	Week 37
9	Tue	
10	Wed	
11	Thu	
12	Fri	
13	Sat	
14	Sun	
15	Mon	Week 38
16	Tue	
17	Wed	
18	Thu	
19	Fri	
20	Sat	
21	Sun	
22	Mon	Week 39
23	Tue	
24	Wed	
25	Thu	
26	Fri	
27	Sat	
28	Sun	
29	Mon	Week 40
30	Tue	

2014   OKTOBER OCTUBRE OTTOBRE OCTOBRE OKTOBER **OCTOBER**

1	Wed	
2	Thu	
3	Fri	
4	Sat	
5	Sun	
6	Mon	Week 41
7	Tue	
8	Wed	
9	Thu	
10	Fri	
11	Sat	
12	Sun	
13	Mon	Week 42
14	Tue	
15	Wed	
16	Thu	
17	Fri	
18	Sat	
19	Sun	
20	Mon	Week 43
21	Tue	
22	Wed	
23	Thu	
24	Fri	
25	Sat	
26	Sun	
27	Mon	Week 44
28	Tue	
29	Wed	
30	Thu	
31	Fri	

1	Sat	
2	Sun	
3	Mon	Week 45
4	Tue	
5	Wed	
6	Thu	
7	Fri	
8	Sat	
9	Sun	
10	Mon	Week 46
11	Tue	
12	Wed	
13	Thu	
14	Fri	
15	Sat	
16	Sun	
17	Mon	Week 47
18	Tue	
19	Wed	
20	Thu	
21	Fri	
22	Sat	
23	Sun	
24	Mon	Week 48
25	Tue	
26	Wed	
27	Thu	
28	Fri	
29	Sat	
30	Sun	

1	Mon	Week 49
2	Tue	
3	Wed	
4	Thu	
5	Fri	
6	Sat	
7	Sun	
8	Mon	Week 50
9	Tue	
10	Wed	
11	Thu	
12	Fri	
13	Sat	
14	Sun	
15	Mon	Week 51
16	Tue	
17	Wed	
18	Thu	
19	Fri	
20	Sat	
21	Sun	
22	Mon	Week 52
23	Tue	
24	Wed	
25	Thu	
26	Fri	
27	Sat	
28	Sun	
29	Mon	Week 1
30	Tue	
31	Wed	

Notes Notizen Notes Note Apuntes Notities

Notes Notizen Notes Note Apuntes Notities

Notes Notizen Notes Note Apuntes Notities

Notes Notizen Notes Note Apuntes Notities

Notes Notizen Notes Note Apuntes Notities

Notes Notizen Notes Note Apuntes Notities

Notes Notizen Notes Note Apuntes Notities

Notes Notizen Notes Note Apuntes Notities

Notities Apuntes Note Notes Notizen **Notes**

Notes Notizen Notes Note Apuntes Notities

Notes Notizen Notes Note Apuntes Notities

Notes Notizen Notes Note Apuntes Notities

Notes Notizen Notes Note Apuntes Notities

Notes Notizen Notes Note Apuntes Notities

Notes Notizen Notes Note Apuntes Notities

Notities Apuntes Note Notes Notizen **Notes**

Notes Notizen Notes Note Apuntes Notities

Notities Apuntes Note Notes Notizen **Notes**

Notes Notizen Notes Note Apuntes Notities

Notes Notizen Notes Note Apuntes Notities

Notes Notizen Notes Note Apuntes Notities

Notes Notizen Notes Note Apuntes Notities

Notes Notizen Notes Note Apuntes Notities

Notes Notizen Notes Note Apuntes Notities

Notes Notizen Notes Note Apuntes Notities

International Trade Abbreviations Internationale Abkürzungen
Abréviations Commerciales

a.a.r.	against all risks, Versicherung gegen alle Gefahren
a/c	a conto, account, Rechnung
A/C	account current, Kontokorrent
A/T	American terms (insurance)
acct.	account, Rechnung
Av.	average, Havarie, Schaden
B.L., B/L	Bill of lading, Schiffsfrachtbrief
c.a.d. (c/d)	cash against documents, Zahlung gegen Dokumente
c.a.f.	cost, assurance, freight included, Kosten, Versicherung, Fracht
cf., c.f., c&f	cost and freight, Kosten und Fracht
c.i., c&i	cost and insurance, Einstandspreis und Versicherung
C/I	certificate of insurance, Versicherungspolice
C.I.A.	cash in advance, Zahlung im Voraus
c.i.f.	cost, insurance, freight included, Kosten, Versicherungsprämie, Fracht eingeschlossen
c.i.f. & c.	cost, insurance, freight & commission
c.i.f. +	Kommission
c.i.f.c & i.	cost, insurance, freight, commission & interest
c.i.f.c. +	Bankzinsen
c.o.d., cod	cash collect on delivery, Zahlung bei Auslieferung oder Empfang
c.o.s.	cash on shipment, Zahlung bei Verschiffung
C.W.O.	cash with order, Zahlung mit Anweisung
D.A., D/A	documents against acceptance, Dokumente gegen Akzeptierung einer Tratte
D.A.D.	documents against disposition, Dokumente gegen Verfügung (über Ladung)
d.f.	dead freight, Fautfracht für nicht genutzten Laderaum
D/N	debit note, Lastschrift
D.O. (D/o)	delivery order, Auslieferungsanweisung
d/p	documents against payment, Dokumente gegen Zahlung
D/W	dock warrant, Ladeplatz-Berechtigung
E.c.	English conditions (insurance), Englische Bedingungen (Versicherung)
E.O.M.	end of month, zum Monatsende
F	first class, Erster Klasse
f.a.a., faa	free of all average, frei von jedem Schaden
f.a.s.	free alongside ship, frei Längsseite Schiff
f.b.h.	free on board at harbor, frei an Bord im Hafen
F & D	freight and demurrage, Fracht und Liegegeld
F.F.A.	free from alongside, frei von Längsseite her
Fgt. (frt.)	freight, Fracht
f.i.o.	free in and out, frei Ein- und Ausladen und Löschen
f.o.a.	free on aircraft, frei an Bord des Flugzeugs
f.o.b., fob	free on board, frei an Bord
f.o.c.	free on charge, frei an Belastung, Forderung
f.o.d.	free of damage, frei von Schaden
f.o.q.	free on quay, frei auf Kai
f.o.r.	free on rail, frei Bahnhof oder auf Güterwagen
FOR	free on road, frei bis Straße
f.o.s.	free on ship, frei ins Schiff
f.o.t.	free on truck, frei auf Güterwagen, LKW oder Bahnhof
f.o.w.	free on wagon, frei auf Güterwagen
f.p.a.	free of particular average, frei von Beschädigung, außer Strandungsfall
frt. pp.	freight prepaid, Fracht bezahlt
g.a., G/A	general average, große Havarie, großer Schaden
I.B.	in bond, unverzollte Ware unter Zollverschluss
int.	interests, Bankzinsen
i.p.a.	including particular average, Beschädigung von Waren eingeschlossen
i.t.	immediate transport, sofortiger, unmittelbarer Transport
L/C	letter of credit, Kreditbrief, Akkreditiv
L.&D.	loss and damage, Verlust und Schaden
M.D.	month's date, Monatsdatum
M.I.P	marine insurance policy, See-Versicherungspolice
M/P	months after payment, Zahlung nächsten Monat
M/R	mate's receipt, Quittung des Landungsoffiziers über Empfang der Ware an Bord
N	night-flight, Nachtflug
N/t	new terms, neue Vertragsbedingungen
n.wt.	net weight, Nettogewicht
O.P.	open floating policy (insurance), offene oder laufende Police
O.R.D.	owner's risk of damage, Eigners Gefahr bei Schaden
O/T	old terms, alte Vertragsbedingungen
P/a	particular average, besondere Beschädigung von Waren durch Transportunfälle
pd.	paid, Bezahlung
P.L.	partial loss, Teilschaden
P/N	promissory note, Eigen-, Solawechsel
P.O.D.	pay on delivery, Zahlung bei Lieferung, Zustellung
ppd.	prepaid, Vorauszahlung
ppt.	promptly, sofort liefer- und zahlbar
rect. (rept.)	receipt, Eingang der Ware, Empfang
R.I.	reinsurance, Rückversicherung
RP	reply paid, Rückzahlung
S.&F.A.	shipping and forwarding agent, Schiffsspediteur
s.g. (sp.gr.)	specific gravity, spezifisches Gewicht, Gewichte
S/N	shipping note, Schiffszettel
T/A	trade acceptance, Handelsakzept
t.l.o., T.L.O.	total loss only, Totalverlust
t.q.	trade quality, Handelssorte, Handelsqualität
tr.	tare, Tara
uc	usual conditions, gewöhnliche Bedingungen
u.t.	usual terms, übliche Vertragsbedingungen
U/w	underwriter, Versicherer
W.B.	way bill, Versandavis, Bordero, Frachtkarte, Frachtbrief
w.g.	weight guaranteed, garantiertes Gewicht
w/m, W/M	weight or measurement, Maß oder Gewicht
wpa	with particular average, mit Teilschaden, d. h. jede Beschädigung ist vom Versicherer zu ersetzen
W.R.	war risk, Kriegsrisiko
W/R	warehouse receipt, Lagerhausbescheinigung
wt	weight, Gewicht
W/W	warehouse warrant, Lagerhausberechtigung

*without guarantee